SYRIA

Martin Gostelow

JPMGUIDES

Contents

This Way Syria

First in the Field

Why visit Syria, and why just now? The reasons are compelling. The celebrated classical ruins of Palmyra in the midst of the desert, the mighty Crusader fortress of Krak des Chevaliers, the historic cities of Damascus and Aleppo—all live up to their billing as wonders of the world. Add to this the comforting fact that Syria is a safe and friendly country. As yet there are few visitors: at sites which ought to be world-famous, you may be quite alone. Persistent Middle Eastern troubles have put people off, even though Syria itself is peaceful.

Bounded to the west by the Mediterranean and Lebanon, to the south by Israel and Jordan, to the east by Iraq, and to the north by Turkey, Syria's location in the Middle East could not be more strategic. The Fertile Crescent, a great arc of rich, well-watered land along the valleys of the Euphrates and the Orontes, lies mainly within the borders of Syria. Some 10,000 years ago, say the archaeologists, this is where the human race first settled down, grew crops and built villages and towns. Early forms of writing evolved in the region, first cuneiform, then hieroglyphic and eventually alphabetic—perhaps the single greatest contribution to the spread of knowledge and thus of civilization.

Rivers and Mountains

The Euphrates was one of the four rivers that flowed through the mythical earthly Paradise—*Edinu* to the Babylonians, Eden in the Bible. In the real world, it cuts across the northeast of the vast limestone plateau which forms the greater part of Syria. Much of the plateau is desert or semi-desert, so the green ribbon of the Euphrates valley was often the preferred invasion route of expansionist powers to the east or west.

In the west, the Orontes flows out of the mountains of Lebanon, winding north through the historic cities of Homs and Hama and into Turkey. Its valley, the agricultural heartland of Syria, is framed to the west by the mountain wall of the Jebel an-Nusairiyah, historic home of more than one important minority among the country's mosaic of religious sects. Once the stronghold of the Ismailis (and their sinister-sounding medieval offshoot, the Assassins), it's now better known as the home of the Alawis, formerly

poor and powerless but now influential. Then comes the narrow coastal plain, a much shorter strip since the French detached Lebanon and transferred another important piece of territory to Turkey. Lattakia is Syria's only major seaport.

Two Ancient Cities

Separated from the sea by two mountain ranges, the Lebanon and Anti-Lebanon, Damascus grew up thousands of years ago as a different kind of port—a desert port where caravans from the east and south came to trade. As capital, it has vastly expanded in recent years, but its old centre preserves unique relics of Christian, Roman and Islamic history. Aleppo in the north has traded with east and west for just about as long, and its covered souks are even older and more atmospheric than the capital's.

Most of Syria's 18 million people are concentrated along the north-south axis from Aleppo to Damascus, representing a small fraction of the country's 185,000 sq km (72,000 sq miles) but some of the best agricultural land. The continental climate means baking hot and dry summers and cold winters with rain and snow in the mountains. The coast enjoys a Mediterranean climate: even winter can be pleasant, though interrupted by storms that can last for two or three days. Spring and autumn are perfect times for a visit, in their very different ways. In spring the plains are dressed in the emerald green of young wheat or fresh grazing. Later in the year, you might think the same land was a desert.

In the News

Syria has gained a reputation for its intransigence in international affairs, and for an austere and authoritarian regime at home. But the example of neighbouring Lebanon showed with painful clarity that in the Middle East, the only guarantee of national integrity and peace is to have a strong government. It took Syrian intervention to impose a fragile ceasefire in Lebanon, still valid apart from the southern border with Israel. Syrian opposition to separate deals between its neighbours and Israel has never wavered; it insists on the return of the Golan Heights lost in the 1967 war as part of a general peace settlement. Such an outcome might look a long way off, but Israel knows there can be no real peace until relations with Syria are normalized.

A Warm Welcome

This is a nation proud of its achievements, from the discovery of the secrets of agriculture and metallurgy, the invention of the

The small shops of the souk have scarcely changed in centuries.

alphabet, the birth of the first cities, to the flowering of literature, science and mathematics after the Arab conquest. In modern times there have been other grand schemes, such as the draining of the Ghab marshes and the building of the biggest earth-filled dam in the world, the key to harnessing the Euphrates for electric power and irrigation. But Syrians don't boast; they prefer to let their qualities of tenacity, competence and a taste for scholarship speak for them. They are, in fact, rather shy, dignified and serious, just occasionally allowing their faces to light up with a gentle smile.

If the emphasis on internal security seems rather heavy-handed, take it in your stride. It will be tempered by the warmth of the welcome you'll receive from some of the friendliest people you could wish to meet. Traditional Arab hospitality is alive and well; in a remote village or a big city, you're quite likely to be invited into someone's home for tea or coffee. On the commercial level, too, Syria welcomes visitors. Hotels ranging from comfortable to palatial, several of them members of a locally-owned chain, have opened conveniently close to many of the most famous historic sites.

7

Flashback

Origins

"This is where civilization began!" say the Syrians, and they have a point. About 10,000 BC, in the Fertile Crescent, humans started to settle down and cultivate crops instead of simply collecting seeds and plants in the wild. Gathering together for protection against the nomads of the desert and the mountains, they created their first villages and then walled towns. Trade eventually developed in food surpluses, precious metals and the raw materials for weapons as bronze replaced stone.

By 3000 BC, Mari on the Euphrates had become one of the first known urban civilizations, with powerful rulers—to judge by the extent of the palace ruins. With centralized control, agriculture could be more efficient, and irrigation further multiplied the output. There was now time and wealth to spend on organized religion. And ambitious leaders with spare manpower could turn greedy eyes on their neighbours, then further afield. The world's first armies were on the march.

A door to the past in Aleppo, one of the oldest Middle Eastern cities.

Empire Builders

Successive waves of invaders from Mesopotamia (now Iraq) overran Syria, culminating in about 1750 BC with the Babylonians who sacked Mari on the way. Then came the Hittites from what is now Turkey, to battle with Egypt for supremacy. With the aid of a new technology, the smelting of iron for weapons, the Hittites prevailed.

Around 1000 BC, Aramaeans from Arabia moved in; their language became the everyday speech of the region until the time of Christ and long afterwards. Then history repeated itself when the Assyrians, followed in 612 BC by a new Babylonian kingdom, spread from Mesopotamia and took over. Most efficient of the early autocracies, the Persians conquered Babylon in 539 BC and inherited and enlarged its territories. Two centuries later, Alexander the Great and his Macedonians routed the huge Persian army at Issus, the northern gates of Syria. Within ten years, in 323 BC, Alexander was dead, having built the greatest empire yet. His generals divided it up, with Ptolemy taking Egypt and southern Syria, and Seleucus northern Syria and Mesopotamia.

Romans and Christians

By 64 BC, the Seleucid Empire had fallen apart. The Roman general Pompey marched in, expelled other contenders including the Armenians, and made Syria a Roman province. It was to become one of the richest, and serve as a launching pad for expeditions to the east as one emperor after another tried to emulate Alexander. And when Rome weakened, Syria was to suffer its own share of invasions.

The life and death of Jesus Christ and the journeys of his apostle Paul to Damascus, Antioch and Rome itself were scarcely noticed at the time, but they were eventually to rock the Roman Empire. The first area in the world to become Christian, Syria was riven by disputes—and worse—about the interpretation of the scriptures. Holders of one view accused those with other ideas of heresy. When the empire split, the eastern Byzantine emperors attempted to impose a single approved creed, sometimes by force.

Islamic Conquest

The Prophet Mohammed, founder of Islam, died at Medina in 632. Soon afterwards, his followers swept north out of Arabia in a lightning campaign. The Byzantines, weakened by war with the Persians, were in no condition to put up much resistance. After persecution of their sects under the empire, many of the local Christians were in a mood to welcome the Arab conquerors. In the early years Islam was tolerant of other religions; there was no pressure to convert.

The death of Mohammed was followed by immediate dispute about the leadership. The first successor (or caliph) was Abu Bakr, father of one of the Prophet's wives, in spite of the claim of Ali, his son-in-law. Eventually, Ali succeeded as fourth caliph, but Muawiya, the energetic governor of Syria, opposed him, and after Ali's murder became caliph himself in 661. The supporters of Ali and his son Hussein evolved into the Shia sect of Islam, traditionally opposed to the Sunni national majority.

Muawiya, who was the first of the Omayyad dynasty, transferred the capital to Damascus, where the Omayyads ruled with a light hand; they were patrons of the arts, lovers of music, hunting and wine—all anathema to the stricter Muslims of Arabia and Iraq. In 750, the Omayyads were overthrown by the Abbasids, who moved the caliphate capital to Baghdad.

The Crusades

Whatever your view of the rights and wrongs of the enterprise (and any starry-eyed romanticism is certainly misplaced), the story of the Crusades is a dramatic one. After Muslim armies had taken most of Asia Minor (present-day Turkey) from the Byzantines, the emperor in Constantinople (now Istanbul) appealed for help. In 1095, rabble-rousing French preachers and Pope Urban II called for a "crusade" to go to the aid of fellow Christians in the East. Knights, foot-soldiers and a host of camp followers, perhaps 100,000 in all, set out to cross Europe and Asia Minor. Their motives were, to say the least, mixed. Some were certainly high-minded; far more were in it for adventure, loot and land.

Many died or deserted on the way, but a year and a half later, the remnant entered Syria. Capturing Antioch in 1098, they marched south via Homs, down to the coast and up to the walls of Jerusalem. After a six-week siege, they took the city and, in an orgy of bloodlust, massacred most of the inhabitants—Muslims, Jews and many of the Christian community as well.

The Crusaders seized a strip of land from southern Turkey down the Mediterranean coast and across to the Red Sea. A second crusade tried to take Damascus in 1148 but ended in fiasco. From then on, reinforcements from Europe were always too few and the Crusader states had to seek refuge in stone. Often on the sites of Byzantine and Arab fortifications, they took the art of castle-building to new heights, creating massive fortresses, manned mainly by the orders of religious knights, the Templars and Hospitallers. They were helped, too, by division among the Muslims, until a leader emerged to unite them: the Kurdish general Salah al-Din, known to the West as Saladin. Crushing the Crusader army in 1187, he retook Jerusalem and many of the coastal towns and castles. A third crusade, with Richard the Lion-Heart at its head, stopped the rot. A century later, after other ineffectual crusades, the ruthless Mameluke sultans finally expelled the Crusaders from their last footholds in the East.

Turkish Empire

By the early 16th century, the Ottoman sultans had come to power in Constantinople and made themselves masters of the Mediterranean. In 1516 they beat the Mamelukes and took control of Syria. Aleppo and Damascus did well from trade and the pilgrims on their way to Mecca. Later, the Ottoman Turks ruled through local pashas, some of them efficient, many lazy and corrupt. Early in the 19th century, Mohammed Ali, Pasha of Egypt, 11 rejected Turkish rule. His son Ibrahim seized Syria in 1832 and began to modernize the administration. Although the Turks returned within ten years, there was a gradual opening to the West, bringing wider educational and travel opportunities. One of the effects was the rebirth of Arab nationalism.

When World War I broke out in 1914, Turkey joined in as an ally of Germany. It suited Britain to encourage the Arabs living under Turkish rule to revolt, and in 1916 the Arabs of the Hejaz (Saudi Arabia) rose against the Turks. The British advanced from Egypt into Palestine, and Arab irregulars advised by T.E. Lawrence raided behind Turkish lines. The Turks were forced to retreat and in 1918, British troops under General Allenby and Arab forces led by the Emir Faisal entered Damascus. A Syrian assembly elected Faisal king of Syria, but the victorious western Allies had other plans.

French Mandate

In spite of implying support for their independence to the leaders of the Arab Revolt, Britain had already, in 1916, made a secret agreement with France to carve up the Turkish Empire. The British "sphere of influence" would be Iraq, Trans-Jordan and Palestine. French interests would be paramount in Syria and Lebanon. What this would mean in practice was left vague, but France took it as a licence to impose direct rule. The French army landed in Lebanon and marched on Damascus, which they occupied on 25 July 1920. The Emir Faisal was forced to flee; Britain later installed him as king of Iraq.

Strikes, demonstrations and uprisings punctuated the quarter-century of French rule, and there was a major rebellion in 1925 in the Jebel Druze region in the far south which they never succeeded in quelling. But they did introduce improvements in administration, agriculture, health and education. In 1939, France gave the northern coastal province of Syria to Turkey as a bribe to persuade the Turks not to ally themselves with Germany again. Known as the Sanjak of Alexandretta, the territory included the historic city of Antioch (Antakya) and the port of Iskenderun. Syrians have never been reconciled to the loss: their maps still show the area as part of Syria.

When France was defeated by Nazi Germany in 1940, the French authorities in Syria supported the Vichy government. British and Free French forces invaded and quickly overcame any resistance. The Free French government promised independence but then tried to hang on to power, even bombarding Damascus until stopped by their British allies.

Independence

Independence came in 1946, despite French attempts to retain control. The early years were hard. The UN vote to set up the state of Israel on Palestinian land united the Arab world in opposition, but a Syrian volunteer force sent to fight in the 1948 Arab-Israel war suffered a quick defeat. This signalled the start of a long period of instability, with frequent changes of government and military coups d'état.

The desire for Arab unity led Syria to join with Egypt in 1958 to form the United Arab Republic. It was supposed to be a union of equals, but after the initial euphoria wore off, Syria found that power was all concentrated in Cairo. After an army coup in Damascus in 1961, the partnership was dissolved.

The Baath (Rebirth) Party took over in 1963. Nominally socialist and Arab nationalist, it was actually more pragmatic and dedicated to Syrian interests. The 1967 war with Israel led to the loss of the Golan Heights, and discredited the civilian politicians. In 1970, the air force general Hafiz al-Assad came to power, becoming president in in 1971.

Egypt and Syria attacked Israel in 1973 to try to recover lost territory. Initial gains were soon reversed, but after the cease-fire Syria could at least point to the recovery of the town of Quneitra, albeit in ruins. Syria sent troops to impose a ceasefire in the Lebanese civil war and keeps them there to preserve the peace—avoiding the border near Israel.

The collapse of the Soviet Union deprived Syria of its chief ally and arms supplier. At the same time, lining up with the coalition against Saddam Hussein's Iraq in the 1991 Gulf War opened a channel of communication with the United States.

President Hafiz al-Assad died on June 10, 2000. Until 1994, when he was killed in a car crash, Assad's elder son Basil had been his father's favourite to succeed. The less charismatic younger son Bashar was then promoted as heir-apparent and duly acclaimed as president. He seemed ready to tolerate greater freedom of expression, but disputes with the US over the 2003 Iraq war brought the return of the old defensive attitudes. Syria removed its troops from the Lebanon in April 2005. A peace settlement with Israel still seems as far off as ever, but in Middle Eastern affairs you can never say never. In the meantime, amidst the turmoil of the region, Syria enjoys relative calm.

13

On the Scene

Most visitors to Syria begin their journey in the capital, Damascus. Situated between the mountains and the desert, at a crossroads of ancient trade routes, it was famed through the ages for its surrounding orchards—likened to a halo round the moon. To travellers coming from the arid sands to the east, it seemed like an earthly paradise.

▶ DAMASCUS AND ENVIRONS
The Old City, National Museum,
Tekiyeh as-Sulaimaniyeh Mosque, Excursions

The Syrian capital asserts that it is the oldest continuously inhabited city on earth, with its old rival Aleppo the only other likely candidate. Mentioned in 4,000-year-old clay tablets from Mari, it's among the places listed as conquered by Pharaoh Tuthmosis III in the 15th century BC. In the Bible it appears as the Aramaean capital, in about 900 BC. Assyrians, Babylonians, Persians, Alexander the Great and his successors, Nabataeans from Petra, Romans and Byzantines then ruled in turn. Soon after the death of the Prophet Mohammed, his followers burst out of Arabia and briefly occupied Damascus in AD 635. The following year they returned, after crushing the Byzantine army at the Battle of Yarmouk, and this time it was to stay. In 661 the Omayyad caliphs made the city the capital of the Arab empire which reached from the Atlantic to the Persian Gulf. But its glory lasted only until 750, when the Abbasids moved the capital to Baghdad.

Crusader attacks failed to take Damascus, but it was looted and partly destroyed in successive Mongol invasions. Under the Ottoman Turks, it became the main assembly point for pilgrims on the way to Mecca—a role which has declined in recent years with the growth of charter flights.

The Old City
Modern Damascus, with 2.5 million people, is criss-crossed by broad avenues and ringed by 15

sprawling suburbs, but at its heart, the Old City is a marvel, full of monuments from many periods. Its 13th-century ramparts mainly followed the line of the Roman wall, but they were later neglected and houses were built jutting up against them. Only parts are still visible, but seven of the eight Roman gates can still be found, in various states of preservation.

At first sight a labyrinth, the Old City's souks and alleys actually follow the ancient rectangular street pattern, so it's not too difficult to navigate. The best way—in places the only way—to see it is on foot.

The Citadel

A useful landmark not far from the modern city centre, the 13th-century citadel makes a good place to start. An Arab fortress on Roman foundations, it was neglected by the Turks, although part was used until modern times as a prison. The walls have had a recent facelift, but the inside has been closed for years; a look through the locked gates reveals nothing but a building site.

Souk al-Hamidiyeh

Right next to the citadel is the opening to a long covered market, its high, curved roof of corrugated iron peppered by holes that let in shafts of daylight. Lined with clothing and fabric shops and stores selling every sort of craft and souvenir, the souk is usually thronged with locals, soldiers, villagers from outside Damascus and pilgrims seeing the sights. Traders call to the handful of tourists, offering table-cloths and brass trays, but they're not too pressing. On Fridays, the shops close and hawkers take over, spreading their wares on the ground.

If you divert to the right, just where there's a break in the roof, you'll find a white archway on the left leading to a lovely courtyard. This was the Nur ed-Din Hospital, opened in 1154, and is now the Museum of Arab Science and Medicine.

Continuing along the Souk al-Hamidiyeh, you'll suddenly find yourself amid massive marble columns, Corinthian capitals and carved lintels, the remains of the western gateway to the Roman Temple of Jupiter. Emerging into the daylight, you enter a newly paved square. Facing you is the western wall of the Great Mosque. Massive though it is, this is only the short side of the huge building.

The Great Mosque (Omayyad Mosque)

Sacred since early times, this was the site of the Aramaean temple to the sun god, Hadad. The Ro-

16

mans identified Hadad with Jupiter, and built a colossal new temple in the 1st and 2nd centuries AD. With the Christianization of the empire, it became the cathedral of St John the Baptist.

The first Omayyad caliphs allowed Christians to continue worshipping in the church; part of the enclosure was allocated to Muslims. In about 705, the less tolerant Caliph al-Walid ordered its reconstruction as a mosque—

THE FIVE PILLARS OF ISLAM

A Muslim has five all-important duties to perform.
- The profession of the faith: "There is no god but God (Allah), and Mohammed is His Prophet".
- Prayer five times a day, facing Mecca, culminating in a prostration, the forehead touching the ground.
- The giving of alms to the poor, both as a regular tithe, and spontaneously.
- Strict abstinence in all matters, including food or drink, from sunrise to sunset during Ramadan, the ninth month of the Islamic calendar.
- The pilgrimage to Mecca (the Haj) should be undertaken at least once in a lifetime by all those in good health and having sufficient means.

the greatest place of warship that had ever been built (or, he vowed, ever would be). Using the walls and many columns from the cathedral, the work took just ten years.

The usual entrance is on the north side, near a restored Byzantine colonnade. The courtyard is vast, and on the walls surrounding it, green and gold mosaics depict landscapes and palaces, orchards and streams. Were the artists depicting Paradise? Or Damascus as it then was? Some of the mosaics, near the western entrance, are original 8th-century work, others date from the 13th century. Still more are modern: large parts of the mosque had to be rebuilt after a fire in 1893. The little domed building on eight columns with Corinthian capitals is the Treasury (Al Khazneh).

In the depths of the prayer hall, a small domed shrine is said to house the head of St John the Baptist (known as Yahia to Muslims), the very same head that Herod offered to Salome after she danced for him. A shrine to the Shia martyr Hussein in a chamber at the eastern end attracts pilgrims, many from Iran, the women in all-enveloping black robes.

The mosque has three very different minarets: according to Muslim tradition the highest, the Minaret of Jesus, is where Christ will return to do battle with the Antichrist before the last judgement.

Tomb of Saladin

Salah al-Din, known to the West as Saladin, united the Muslim world against the invading Crusaders. His mausoleum, built in 1193, stands outside the Great Mosque near its northwest corner. It was restored at the end of the 19th century at the expense of Kaiser Wilhelm II of Germany after he had paid a visit.

Returning to the square to the west of the mosque, cross over and turn right to find the mausoleum of Sultan Baibars, the 13th-century Mameluke warrior whose victories fatally weakened the Crusaders.

The narrow street on the south side of the mosque is lined by antique shops and cafés—pay a visit in the evening and you'll see them packed with men playing backgammon and smoking *narghileh* pipes.

Azem Palace

Just a little way down the narrow street leading from the southwest corner of the Great Mosque stands a veritable jewel of 18th-century Damascene architecture, a palace built for Assad Pasha Azem, a governor of Damascus. Extravagantly decorated rooms and alcoves ramble round a garden courtyard, a refuge from the heat and dust of the city. Some of the rooms house exhibits of the Museum of Arts and Popular Traditions, including good displays of embroidered costumes, glass and furniture.

Emerging from the palace, turn left to pass the entrance to the Khan Assad Pasha. A *khan* was an inn and warehouse for visiting merchants and this is one of the finest of many in the Old City.

The Street Called Straight

Now known as Souk al-Tawil (and also as Souk Madhat Pasha), this was the Roman Via Recta, the main east-west thoroughfare mentioned in the New Testament (Acts 9: 11). It was to a house on this street that Saul of Tarsus—the future St Paul—was taken after he was blinded when he "saw the light" on the road to Damascus.

The midpoint, a main crossroads of those days, is marked by a rebuilt Roman arch, and although the street's stately colonnades have vanished, many of today's little shops undoubtedly occupy the houses that stood behind them. At the eastern end, Bab Sharqi (Eastern Gate) is the restored 2nd-century Roman gateway. Turn left just before the gate to find the Chapel of Ananias, named after the man who

Damascus, one of the world's oldest continually inhabited cities.

laid his hands on Paul to bring back his sight. Steps from a courtyard lead down to an ancient cellar. Through the Bab Sharqi and along the wall to the right, St Paul's Chapel is modern, but claims to stand on the site where Paul was let down in a laundry basket to escape from the city.

National Museum

Outside the Old City, northwest of the Citadel, the National Museum of Syria houses an incredibly rich collection of antiquities from every era. Ideally, it should be visited both before and after you travel round the country to see the sites where the treasures

were found. The museum's gardens give a foretaste with their scattered sculptures and stone fragments, and the striking north facade incorporates the stuccoed gate of Qasr al-Hir al-Gharbi, brought from an 8th-century Omayyad palace in the desert west of Palmyra.

Inside, most of the rooms are devoted to a single site or culture. From Ugarit come sculptures, including the ivory head of a prince (seen on Syrian banknotes), cuneiform tablets including some with the royal seal, and a clay tablet with probably the world's first practical alphabet. From Mari, there's superb jew- 19 ellery, some of it a gift from the king of Ur, in southern Mesopotamia.

Other rooms hold impressive Greek and Roman statuary, glass and mosaics, Islamic swords, ceramics and coins. A magnificent mausoleum has been brought here from Palmyra and reassembled, complete with all its sculptures.

Synagogue of Doura Europos

Removed from its site beside the Euphrates (see p. 51) and reconstructed in the museum grounds, this unique place of worship dates from around AD 165. It's remarkable for its wall-paintings of scenes from the Old Testament: Pharaoh's daughter with Moses, the Crossing of the Red Sea, Solomon anointing David, and many more. Human or animal images were generally forbidden in Jewish places of worship. It's a puzzle why this exception was permitted.

Tekiyeh as-Sulaimaniyeh Mosque

Next to the National Museum, a little nearer the Old City and beside the Barada river (above ground at this point but sadly in need of a clean-up), this fine 16th-century mosque was the first built by the Ottoman Turks. It's a symphony of arches, domes and slim minarets, set among gardens ornamented with pools and fountains. Near the main courtyard and mosque, a smaller arcaded courtyard houses a craft centre featuring a glassblowers' workshop.

Military Museum

The Tekiyeh Mosque's gardens make a strange setting for a collection of military hardware and junk, including pieces of aircraft shot down in the 1973 war with Israel. Historic MiG and Sukhoi jet fighters supplied by the Soviet Union stand half-hidden among the trees. Inside part of what was once a *khan* for pilgrims are collections of medieval swords, helmets and chain mail, impressive but not well labelled.

Excursions

A handful of villages in the mountains near Damascus are popular destinations for excursions. At an altitude of 1,200 m (4,000 ft) and more, the clean air, cool streams and orchards bring crowds escaping the summer heat of the city. Two of the most picturesque villages have adhered to Christianity ever since soon after the time of Christ; they shelter famous shrines.

Seydnaya

The village spreads over a rocky hilltop, its summit crowned by the domes and cupolas of a fortress-like convent, founded in the 6th century, although the present buildings date from much later. Within its walls, a chapel of the Virgin Mary is reached by a labyrinth of passages; as in a mosque, you must take off your shoes before entering. The smoke-blackened walls are covered by equally dark paintings, but the focus of adoration is a shrine in the wall, where a half-hidden, indecipherable icon of the Virgin is said to have been painted by St Luke.

Maalula

On the slopes of the Anti-Lebanon, just over 40 km (25 miles) north of Damascus by the motorway, a turn left leads to a village of blue and white houses clinging to the steep slopes beneath a towering cliff face. Most of the people are Greek Catholic, and older inhabitants can still speak some Aramaic, the language used by Jesus Christ. Few of the younger people understand it, but it survives in the phrases of religious ritual.

At the monastery of Mar Sarkis (St Sergius) high above the village, you duck through a low doorway in the modern courtyard to find a 7th-century church. Part of it, cut into the solid rock, may be even older. Icons of St Sergius and St Bacchus, two of Syria's own saints, include one striking image of the hands of God reaching to shield them.

Sheltering under the cliff are the modern buildings of the convent of Mar Tekla (St Thecla), but a cave cut in the cliff above is said to have been the saint's cell. The water dripping from the roof is collected in a font—it is credited with healing powers.

You can climb from the convent to the cliff top by way of a narrow gorge, which would be considered a beauty spot had it not been sadly desecrated by rubbish and graffiti. Even so, it's worth the short walk—notice the water channel cut high on the side of the gorge.

Zabadani

In Damascus itself, the Barada river may be an open or buried sewer, but it still flows cold and fresh out of the Anti-Lebanon mountains. The villages dotting its banks have long provided a summer escape from the city, and now that more people have cars they flock to their favourite picnic spots. One is the little lake near Zabadani, which is identified as the source of the Barada. In summer a little train makes the 50-km (31-mile) journey, but it takes three hours and is likely to be crowded. So is the road: the return to Damascus on Friday evening can create traffic chaos. 21

Southeast of Damascus, the fertile plain of the Hauran was a major wheat-growing region in the days of the Roman Empire, in spite of the back-breaking effort needed to clear fields of the black basalt stone scattered over its surface. Dark outcrops of the same rock mark the way to the massive Jebel Druze (Druze Mountain) to the southeast. The mountain has been officially re-labelled Jebel al-Arab, but the old name persists.

Shahba

At first sight it's an unremarkable, even ugly, town. But the road from Damascus, 88 km (55 miles) away, passes the remnant of a Roman arch, the old north gate, and at the town centre you can make out the rectangular plan of Roman streets. This was Philippopolis, founded by Philip the Arab, who was born in these parts and rose through the ranks of the Roman army until he was hailed as emperor by his legions in AD 244. He died in 249, and the city he began was never finished.

Along a street paved with the original stones, west of the centre, are the remains of the palace, temple and a well-preserved theatre. On the east side of the main street stand two high arches, a remnant of the huge Roman baths. Along a little side street next to the baths, a small museum displays some fine 3rd- and 4th-century mosaics discovered in the town, including a beautiful head of Thetis. They are among the most detailed to be seen in Syria. Others from Shahba have been moved to the museums in Damascus and Suweida.

Suweida

The capital of the Hauran has prospered lately. Fancy modern villas sprawl across the hillside, and not much is left of its origins as a Nabataean town and then the Roman Dionysias. Not much, that is, until you find the grandiose, domed museum, a short way from the middle of town on the road to Qanawat. The star exhibits are detailed, complete mosaics from Shahba, but just as rewarding are the displays on the geology of the Hauran and Jebel al-Arab, and finds from the numerous ancient settlements in the area. Evocative old photographs show Roman buildings that survived into the 20th century, only to be lost through neglect. As the museum illustrates, today's attitude is one of pride in this past and determination to preserve what does remain.

Bosra's Roman theatre, in a remarkable state of preservation.

Qanawat

Only 8 km (5 miles) from Suweida, an ancient settlement (Kenath in the Old Testament) became an important Roman town. On the heights above the modern town, the remains of Roman and Byzantine ramparts surround the village, an early Christian basilica with magnificent sarcophagi, a Roman temple and water cisterns, as well as a wealth of ancient walls incorporated in the houses of the Druze families living here.

Salkhad

East of Suweida, a die-straight road heads directly for a volcanic outcrop crowned by an Arab fortress, probably 12th century in origin but used by every occupying army since. The view from the top is worth the climb, and one of the local boys may be on hand to guide you through the dark maze of vaults and chambers. Don't try it on your own— you could drop through an unseen opening into one of the dungeons, terrifying black holes deep inside the ruins.

Bosra

Already ancient when Emperor Trajan made it the capital of the Roman province of Arabia in AD 106, Bostra, as it was called, became a major metropolis of the 23 empire. Headquarters of a Roman legion, a prosperous crossroads for trade and later the seat of an archbishop, it was equipped with imposing public buildings to match. Bosra's location made it the first prize taken in the Arab conquest, and its mosques and their minarets are among the oldest in Islam.

Theatre and Citadel
On the southern edge of the old town, the Roman theatre is amazingly well preserved, thanks to having been turned into an Arab fortress a thousand years after it was built. Surrounded by an outer wall and bastions (with dozens of classical columns used for reinforcement), the theatre itself was partly filled with earth and rubble. Other buildings were erected on top and, as old French aerial photographs show, only the uppermost seven rows of seats were left exposed. The theatre was excavated in the 1930s, revealing the lower tiers of seats, mostly in excellent condition, together with vestiges of the stage. Now all 37 rows, able to seat about 15,000, rise with giddying steepness to the sky, rimmed by Doric columns, and the stage has been rebuilt. The acoustics remain faultless; a stage whisper can be heard anywhere in the house.

A Walk Through the Town
The world forgot antique Bosra and it dwindled into a backwater.

THE DRUZES
One of the stranger sects that broke away from Islam, the Druzes are not generally regarded as Muslims at all. Their beliefs are kept secret, even from the majority of Druze people themselves, and revealed only to a handful of elders, distinguished-looking gentlemen in cylindrical turbans and baggy trousers. They revere the Caliph Hakim who ruled in Cairo from 996 until his assassination in 1021. (Mainstream Muslims reckon he was insane.) No outsider is permitted to become a Druze, and marriage with a non-Druze is banned. So even if the Druzes didn't start out as a single clan, they have become one.

Often finding themselves outnumbered, they long ago adopted a policy of avoiding trouble with the ruling power, whoever it was. Only if directly threatened would they fight—and then they fought like tigers. Apart from the Jebel Druze, small numbers live across the border in northern Israel, and more in the Lebanon mountains south of Beirut.

A dusty village grew up on the site, making use of the old buildings. Massive columns have been incorporated into the walls of houses, and some door lintels carry part of an engraved inscription. Until a few years ago, the streets were on a level with the doorsteps of the houses. Now some of them have been excavated down to the original Roman paving, in some places 2 m (7 ft) below the surface.

Just to the north of the fortress-theatre, a triple arch dates from the 3rd century. To the east of the arch are the extensive remains of the Roman baths, next to the intersection of the main streets, the *decumanus* running east-west and the *cardo* leading north. Four slim columns at the junction were part of the *nymphaeum*, a water fountain, and behind them is a large market building. Follow the cardo, and on the left after 300 m (330 yd), you'll come to the Mosque of Omar with its square minaret. It may have been begun soon after the Arab conquest in 635 but most probably dates mainly from the early 8th century (like the Great Mosque in Damascus), with many later modifications. The whole building, like so much of Bosra, uses stones from ancient structures.

In a parallel street to the east, the 11th-century Mosque of Fatima has a slim, square minaret like the Mosque of Omar. Facing it are the sadly depleted remains of the 5th-century Christian cathedral.

To the north of the cathedral, not much is left of a Christian basilica called the Church of Bahira by Muslims: according to tradition, the Prophet came here as a boy and a monk, Bahira, predicted his future greatness.

The *decumanus* ends at a triumphal arch, thought to be Nabataean in origin. Walk south and you will come to a huge rectangular reservoir, 155 m long and 122 m wide (170 x 134 yd), and 7 m (23 ft) deep, built by the Romans to store up to three years' water supply.

Deraa

Thronged with international truck traffic, the Syrian side of the border crossing to Jordan offers no reasons to linger. It's notorious as the place where in 1917 T.E. Lawrence claimed to have been seized by the Turks, beaten and sexually assaulted by their commandant, the Bey. The scene is described in *Seven Pillars of Wisdom* and depicted in the film *Lawrence of Arabia*. But the evidence is overwhelming that it never happened. Lawrence's darker side was guilt-ridden and masochistic, and in this story he fantasized both his humiliation and his heroism.

25

▶ ORONTES VALLEY
Homs, Hama, Masyaf, Apamea, Ebla

The Arabic name for the Orontes is Nahr al-Aassi, the "rebel", because it is the only river in the region to flow north. Rising in the Lebanon mountains, it crosses into Syria near ancient Qadesh, where the Hittite and Egyptian armies met in battle in 1274 BC to determine who should rule the Syrian plain. Pharaoh Ramses II only just escaped capture. Back at home, he shamelessly declared a famous victory. But in truth, the Hittites were left as masters of the field.

Between the mountains to the west and the semi-desert steppe to the east is the rich farmland of the Orontes valley, planted with wheat, cotton, sugar beet, tobacco and fruit trees.

Homs

Syria's third-largest city, an industrial and oil-refining centre, is scarcely a tourist attraction, although it's such an important crossroads that almost all routes will lead you to it at some stage. The old quarter is worth exploring if you have the time.

The east-west Al-Kuwatly Street is the main thoroughfare;

The wheels of Hama keep turning but no longer irrigate the fields.

south of it lies the Old City, where the Al-Nuri Mosque is thought to stand on the foundations of the Baal temple. Near the traffic circle where Al-Kuwatly Street meets the Hama road heading north, you'll find extensive modern souks.

The church of St Elian, east of the souks, has some fine 12th-century frescoes in the crypt (and modern wall-paintings by Romanian artists in the main church). An ancient piece of fabric displayed in Um al-Zinnar church is claimed to be the girdle of the Virgin Mary.

About 500 m (550 yd) up the Hama road, the Mosque of Khalid ibn al-Walid is modern, with shiny metal domes, but holds the tomb of Khalid, son of Caliph al-Walid and the general who led the conquest of Syria in 635–36.

Hama

Now ringed by modern suburbs, the old city lies half-hidden where the Orontes has cut a deep ravine for itself. Before you even spot the river, you'll see Hama's famous wooden water-wheels *(noria)*, almost the only survivors of thousands built all over the medieval Arab empire from Portugal to Baghdad. Driven by the flow of the river, as they

27

turned they lifted water through a half-circle and dropped it into channels carried by arched aqueducts to fountains, gardens and fields.

In the Middle Ages, there were 30 of the wheels here: now no more than a dozen are left, some in the centre, others above and below the town. Fewer still are in working order; a couple are kept running as museum pieces. Late at night, almost the only sounds to be heard in Hama are the groaning of the wheels' wooden bearings and the croaking of frogs.

The riverfront on the east bank has been made into a pleasant park, overlooked by a modern hotel. Facing it across the river is the hilltop site of the ancient citadel, long since stripped of its buildings and now a tree-shaded park. The lively modern town spreads along the river to the south.

Southwest of the citadel, Hama's Great Mosque is a meticulous reconstruction. The original was destroyed in 1982, during the suppression by the Syrian army of an uprising by the Muslim Brotherhood, a fundamentalist organization which had previously staged a series of assassinations of its political opponents. In Hama, the rebels held out for four days until crushed by tanks and artillery with the loss of thousands of lives. Much of the Old City was destroyed, but it has been completely rebuilt.

Masyaf

A ruined but spectacularly sited castle overlooking the Orontes valley, Masyaf was briefly held by the Crusaders. But it became famous as the stronghold of the

---

ILL-FATED FAMILY

Known in Roman times as Emesa, Homs was a centre for the worship of the sun-god Baal (Elagabal). Its years of glory came after Julia Domna, the brilliant daughter of its high priest, married Septimius Severus, who became emperor in AD 193. When he died at York in 211, their sons Caracalla and Geta shared the succession until Caracalla had his brother killed and then terrorized the empire until he, too, was assassinated. In a bizarre episode, Julia Domna's great-nephew Heliogabalus, who had been appointed high priest of Elagabal as a child, was installed as emperor at the age of 14. In Rome, his decadent behaviour soon outraged the Praetorian Guard, who murdered him and put his more rational cousin Alexander Severus on the throne instead.

Assassins (an Ismaili Muslim sect) in the 12th century. Their leader, known to the Crusaders as the "Old Man of the Mountain", defended his territory by sending one or two of his followers to kill actual or prospective enemies, notably sultans and princes. Sometimes the threat alone was enough: even Saladin was deterred. The word *assassin*, now found in many languages, perhaps derived from the belief that the killers were fortified in their zeal by taking hashish.

A market town covers the slopes to the west of the castle, but on the east it stands dramatically high and clear above the river and its valley planted with orchards.

Apamea (Qalaat al-Mudiq)

On a high promontory overlooking the Orontes valley, Apamea was one of the chief cities of the Seleucid Empire, founded by Alexander the Great's general, Seleucus when he inherited most of Alexander's conquests (Ptolemy taking Egypt). Pompey the Great conquered what was left of the Seleucid lands in 64 BC, and Apamea became a Roman city.

Citadel

The first landmark to be seen is the ruined Arab citadel, built on Crusader foundations. The hilltop site has been taken over by the houses and shops of an Arab village. If you drive up there you'll probably be offered some bogus antiquities, but you'll have a good view of the massive ruins of a Roman theatre far below, and the fertile plain where the Seleucid war elephants were supposedly trained.

Ancient City

Below the citadel, another track (anyone will direct you) leads up to a lower and much larger hill, the actual site of Apamea. The excavations mostly follow the line of its north-south main street, the *cardo*, almost 2 km (over a mile) long. Looking at the colonnades which line a large part of it, you may find it hard to believe that until the 1970s, scarcely a single stone stood on top of another. Since then, the restoration of Apamea has been the pet project of Dr Osman Aidi, a Syrian business magnate and philanthropist. The result is remarkably beautiful: fluted spiral columns, alternately twisting one way or the other, the pediments of great temples, intricately carved capitals and friezes—thousands of tonnes of the original stones have been lovingly re-erected. And where filling-in with modern materials was needed, it has been subtly distinguished from the original.

29

A shepherd keeps watch beside the Roman colonnade at Apamea.

Museum

In the village of Qalaat al-Mudiq, below the hill, there's an impressive 16th-century Ottoman *khan*, a lodging house for pilgrims and travelling traders. A fine vaulted building set around a large square courtyard, it now houses a museum of antiquities removed from the local site, notably mosaics from the Byzantine churches. Some of them show gory hunting scenes, from pre-Christian times when the buildings were temples.

Ebla

No-one knew what would be revealed when, in 1964, Italian archaeologists began the excavation of Tell Mardikh, near Idlib. What they found was a Bronze Age city which flourished between 2500 and 1600 BC. In 1975 they discovered 17,000 clay tablets written in a previously unknown Semitic language, plus bilingual tablets that help the painstaking process of translation. Egyptian vases and lapis lazuli from Afghanistan show the extent of Ebla's trade.

The site is one for the specialist: a chequerboard of trenches and the foundations of ambitious buildings. But some of the treasures can be seen in a new museum at Idlib, and others in the National Museum in Aleppo.

A narrow strip of Mediterranean coast between Turkish and Lebanese territory embraces Syria's only ports and its modest beach resorts. Relics remain from 200 years of Crusader occupation, and 25 years of French, but the main impression is of rapid modern development.

Like a wall between the coast and the Orontes valley, the Jebel an-Nusairiyah mountains have been the fortress and refuge of several unorthodox sects, especially the Alawis. Their villages used to be poor and neglected. Now there are plenty of signs of prosperity, such as a host of new chalet-style houses.

Tartus (Tortosa)

The town grew up on the mainland opposite the Phoenician port on the island of Arwad. In the early Christian era, it became a focus of pilgrimage: an icon of the Virgin Mary was credited with miraculous powers. The First Crusade took Tortosa in 1102, and built strong new fortifications, including the coastal citadel, as well as a cathedral dedicated to Our Lady of Tortosa. The Knights Templar took over and improved the defences, holding out in the citadel even when Saladin captured most of the neighbouring strongholds and sacked the town.

Cathedral

The massive cathedral looks like a fortress itself, and indeed it was intended to withstand an attack if need be. When taken by the Muslim reconquest, it was inevitably turned into a mosque (and thus preserved) and has also been a barracks and a cowshed in its time. Now it does duty as a museum of antiquities. But once inside the small west door, you could imagine yourself in a medieval cathedral in France. The style is part Romanesque, in the rounded arches across the nave and the three apses at the eastern end, and part Gothic, in the pointed arches along the side aisles. The centre pier in the colonnade on the north side is cut through by a transverse vault which may once have led to the 4th-century Byzantine chapel harbouring the icon of Our Lady of Tortosa, that existed prior to construction of the cathedral. Stone steps behind the pier now intriguingly lead up to nowhere. The museum exhibits include some good pieces from all eras, but all jumbled together and inadequately labelled.

31

Traces of the Templars

The remains of the citadel are hemmed in by modern construction, but parts of the walls and keep can still be seen facing the sea. Explore the maze of streets behind them and you can find traces of the Templars; part of their banqueting hall stands against the north wall of what used to be the inner enclosure, now a dusty square where old-fashioned village life goes on. Coffee beans roast over a bed of charcoal, children play with baby goats.

Arwad

A Phoenician port, this rocky island 3 km (2 miles) offshore was the last fragment of land held by the Crusaders in the east after they fled from Tortosa. They then had to watch as the forces of Sultan Baibars destroyed the town to prevent them from returning. Supplied by sea, they clung to their isle for another 11 years, until 1302.

Now the houses of a fishing village cover the island, re-using ancient stones and obscuring Phoenician and Crusader walls and foundations. The island's harbour is sheltered by two breakwaters, like the pincers of a crab, and launches chug to and fro on the 20-minute trip to Tartus, carrying the residents to work or to market.

KNIGHT FIGHTERS

As the Crusaders ran short of manpower, they began to rely on two orders of knights—in effect military monks—to defend key castles. The Hospitallers (or Knights of the Order of the Hospital of St John of Jerusalem) originally had the duty of caring for sick pilgrims. The Templars (the Poor Knights of Christ and of the Temple of Solomon) had that of protecting pilgrims on their way to the Holy Land. But both orders were soon involved in fighting.

Their vows of obedience made them the Crusaders' most reliable soldiers; unlike others, they didn't go home when the mood took them. Their experience extended to politics as well as war, and they were sometimes suspected of being in league with local Muslim chiefs.

When the Crusaders were finally expelled, the Templars expected to live on their lands in Europe. But they had attracted envy and suspicion by acting as international bankers and becoming immensely rich; their property was seized, their leaders tortured and the order suppressed. The Hospitallers moved to Rhodes, then to Malta, which they defended heroically against the Turks in the 16th century.

Amrit

On the mainland south of Tartus you can spot traces of a temple cut into the solid rock of the hillside in about the 6th century BC. A bit further south and just inland from the old coast road (not the new one on reclaimed land) are two tombs marked by curious monuments of solid stone, one cylindrical with a much-eroded pyramid on top, the other conical with a round top and carved lions on the base. They are thought to be funerary towers dating from the 4th century BC, when the Persian Empire held sway over Syria. Beneath them are rock-cut tombs with side chambers.

Krak des Chevaliers

The only major break in the mountain chain that lines the coast of Syria and Lebanon, the Homs Gap has often been an invasion route—in both directions. So it's no surprise to find castles on guard to the north and south of the gap. The greatest of all medieval fortresses stands 35 km (22 miles) from the sea on an outlying ridge at the southern end of the Jebel an-Nusairiyah. From its perfect vantage point, 300 m (1,000 ft) high, it enjoys a commanding view of the fertile lowlands. In Crusader hands, it could prevent Muslim access to the coast, and act as a base for raids inland.

During his triumphant campaign of 1187–88, in which he picked off one Crusader stronghold after another, Saladin rode up to the Krak to inspect its defences. Deciding that a siege would be long, costly and a failure, he rode away again. At that time it was held by a garrison of up to 2,000, many of them Hospitaller knights, but afterwards the numbers dwindled. When the Mameluke Sultan Baibars besieged it in 1271, there were a mere 200. Even so, they were still holding on after a month of bombardment. Then, the story goes, a letter arrived from the knights' commander in Tripoli. There was no hope of reinforcements, it said, and the defenders should negotiate a surrender. Under a guarantee of safe conduct, they marched out, abandoning the mighty fortress to the Muslim army. Only when they reached Tripoli did they find that the letter had been a forgery.

Attackers' View

The steep road up to the Krak des Chevaliers passes through the village of Qalaat al-Hosn, built to house the hundreds of people who were moved out of the castle in the 1930s by the French authorities. Either before or after going inside, it's worth taking the road which circles round to the west of the castle for the most 33

The formidable Krak—the mightiest of all crusader fortresses.

complete overview—and the definitive photograph. Notice how the most powerful defences guard the castle's weak point, facing the ridge from which attackers might bombard it.

Entrance and Outer Ward

Through the main gate you begin to climb quite steeply towards the heart of the castle by way of a wonderfully complex zig-zag entrance passage. At one point it almost doubles back upon itself, and if you have time (allow at least two hours for your visit), this is where you can make a diversion into the ward between the outer and inner walls. An opening leads down to the moat, where you can look up at the mountainous slope of the stone glacis (or talus), built by the Hospitallers to protect the south wall from collapse through undermining, earthquakes or missiles hurled from the southern ridge.

The Interior

The entrance ramp leads to the main inner court, surprisingly small for so great a fortress but made so by the buildings that were added round its periphery. Facing you is the lovely, vaulted Gothic loggia, and behind it the 12th-century knights' dining hall.

Behind that again is a much longer hall, vaulted right down to the floor and once divided into kitchens and stores. The austere chapel in the northeast corner of the court (to the right of the entrance) has a simple nave and apse in late Romanesque style. At the southern end of the court, massive columns support the roofs of more storehouses and refectories.

Outside steps lead up and up, until eventually you stand at the summit of this man-made mountain, on top of one of the bastions above the glacis. At the pinnacle of their power, the knights in their impregnable castle were commanders of all they could see: by the latter days they must have felt isolated here, cut off by an overwhelmingly superior enemy.

Safita

Like the Krak des Chevaliers, Safita was part of the defences of the Homs Gap, the natural route between the coast and the interior. Visible from afar, only the keep of the White Castle of the Templars survives, standing on a hilltop amid a jumble of houses. But look at the street pattern: it follows the oval line of the castle walls, many fragments of which have been built into later constructions. Safita has a comfortable hotel, a useful base for visiting the Krak des Chevaliers as well.

Marqab (Margat)

Visible from far away, the dark, glowering walls and towers of another great Crusader castle dominate the coast from a hilltop near Baniyas. Like the Krak des Chevaliers, it became a stronghold of the Hospitallers, who were determined to make it impregnable. It held out almost to the last, only surrendering in 1285 when the Mameluke Sultan Qalaun finally undermined its walls with tunnels.

The narrow road up to the castle arrives beneath the eastern wall and continues to the south side, rebuilt by the Mamelukes with decorative marble bands to relieve the black basalt. The way in is by a ramp through the great west gate tower, then by an inner gate to a triangular courtyard, with a Gothic chapel leading off to the side.

The top of the round keep commands an outstanding view of the coast and mountains.

Qirdaha

North of Baniyas on the road to Lattakia, a wide road branches inland and climbs to the village where the late President Hafiz al-Assad was born in 1930. New apartment blocks and elaborate public buildings have transformed it in recent years, and statues, pictures and slogans honour him and his sons Basil and Bashar.

Lattakia

Syria lost its major ports, Beirut and Tripoli, when the French drew the boundary around a separate Lebanon in the 1920s. Old Lattakia became Syria's main outlet to the sea. In recent years it has gone through a period of explosive growth; the population exceeds 200,000.

There isn't a great deal left to suggest that (as Laodicea) this was one of the centres of the Seleucid Empire, nor that it remained an important place under the Romans, Byzantines and Crusaders. A tetrapyle, a gateway with four bays, marks the crossing of the two main streets of the Roman grid, and nearby four columns survive from a colonnade.

Beaches

Most of Syria's Mediterranean beaches suffer from pollution and uncleared rubbish, though they're still popular with the locals. The best of them, to the north of Lattakia, is Shatt al-Azraq. A small "Syrian Riviera", it's the most fashionable and best-maintained. A couple of large resort hotels are packed with local vacationers in summer, but the rest of the year

THE ALAWIS

The Jebel an-Nusairiyah (or Jebel Alawi) mountains have been the home of the mysterious Alawi sect for a thousand years. Springing up in the Shia surge which swept Islam, the Alawis were left isolated when that tide retreated. They share with mainstream Shias the belief that Ali, the Prophet's son-in-law, was robbed of his rightful inheritance, but go further in seeing him as a near-divinity. Denounced for centuries by the majority Sunnis as infidels, they took refuge in secrecy, and in these rugged hills. Every occupying power persecuted them: the Crusaders, the Ismailis (who share the mountains to this day), Saladin and the Mamelukes. Traditionally they had no mosques: they were forced by the Turks to build them.

Under the French mandate things began to change. Following their policy of "Divide and Rule", the French created an Alawi state with a measure of autonomy, even attaching Lattakia to it. They promoted Alawi education and recruited men into a militia. When independence came to Syria, this French connection meant they were viewed with suspicion, so they lay low on the political scene. But many became officers in the armed forces—Hafiz al-Assad himself began as a fighter pilot. When unstable civilian government was replaced by a military regime, many Alawis rose to high-ranking positions.

they can be useful bases for visiting the sites along the coast and the nearby mountains.

Ugarit (Ras Shamra)
On a cape to the north of the beach hotels and 14 km (9 miles) from Lattakia, excavations started by the French in 1929 have revealed one of the world's most ancient cities. Ugarit traded with Cyprus, Egypt and the cities along the Euphrates over 4,000 years ago, becoming one of the main ports of the Phoenicians, a Semitic people who went on to found a trading empire—their colony of Carthage in North Africa was eventually to outlast the motherland and challenge Rome for supremacy. Earlier, around 1400 BC, the world's first alphabetic writing (perhaps first developed in the Sinai) came into use here.

Most of the exciting finds were removed to Paris in the 1930s and, more recently, to the national museums in Damascus and Aleppo. But the *tell*, or mound that built up from layer upon layer of ruins and detritus over thousand of years, has been sliced away to expose the street pattern of the 13th century BC. The remains of stone walls, gates and towers, a palace with a complex water system and many substantial houses give a sense of the importance of the place, now so

tranquil. In cellars beneath many of the houses, the quality of the stonework is superb. The acropolis, the high ground to the north of the main area, was the site of the Phoenician temples; it gives a good overview of the excavation and the seaside setting.

Qalaat Salah ad-Din
An hour's drive inland among the rock-strewn hills of the Jebel an-Nusairiyah, a spur of land is crowned by one of the greatest of the Crusaders' castles. It was known to them as Saône (from the Arabic name of the site, Sahyun), but Syrian maps and road signs call it Qalaat Salah ad-Din, Saladin's Castle, to commemorate its capture by the Muslim hero.

On two sides of a long triangular ridge the ground falls away steeply; the problem was to defend the third side. The solution: a rock-cut channel, more than 150 m (500 ft) long, 28 m (90 ft) deep and up to 20 m (66 ft) across. It was too wide for a single-span bridge so the builders left a needle of stone to support their bridge midway. In all, it is estimated that 200,000 tonnes of rock were excavated. They were not wasted, of course, but used to build the castle's massive defences.

It's a staggering achievement, an echoing, vertical gorge, one 37

More medieval defences at Saône, taken by Saladin in 1188.

side of it blending smoothly into the castle walls which seem to grow out of it. These people meant to stay for ever, you'll conclude. In the event, the Crusader presence was to last a mere 75 years.

Saladin besieged Saône in 1188, using mangonels to throw great stone balls against the walls. Eventually the garrison was so depleted that the attackers were able to scale the ramparts in an undefended sector. Entry today is easier, by a long flight of stone steps that leaves everyone puffing as they reach the gate. For a general view, climb to the top of one of the square towers, typical of

12th-century Crusader fortification; in the 13th they adopted the round tower, as at Krak des Chevaliers.

The road up to Saône heads inland just south of Lattakia. Signs are sporadic; Haffeh is the nearest town to the castle. When in doubt, ask the way—everyone will know where you are going. After the visit, if you have your own transport and it suits your itinerary, a new road can take you east across a high mountain pass and down into the Orontes valley, Hama, Apamea or Aleppo. The view of the Ghab, the former marshes now turned into rich farmland, is breathtaking.

► ALEPPO (HALAB)

Souks and Khans, Great Mosque, Citadel, National Museum, Qalaat Semaan

The point of departure for expeditions eastward, and terminus for the caravan trade with India and China, Aleppo was coveted and fought over by all the early empires before becoming part of the Muslim world. It was accorded near-mythical status in medieval Europe as a source of rich silks and spices. And it was from Aleppo that the Darley Arabian horse, one of only three ancestors from which all thoroughbred racehorses in the West are descended, was taken to England in 1705.

To find the historic area at the heart of today's sprawling modernity, just look for the citadel, a great mound ringed by ramparts which itself stands within the original walled city. The majestic main gate of the citadel faces south; immediately to the west of it are Aleppo's fabled souks, a labyrinth of lively covered markets with a total length of 7 km (4 miles).

Souks and Khans

Daylight enters only through openings in the vaulted ceilings which cover this amazing Aladdin's cave. There's a blaze of electric lights of course, but just imagine when it was lit by candles and oil lamps. With some exceptions—the goldsmiths, the tailors—the tradition of one street, one trade has largely vanished. Now butchers are next to shoe shops, nut sellers and perfumers. The aromas of spices and appetizing cooking fill the air.

If you can persuade a shopkeeper to allow you up one of the little stairways to the rooftop, you'll find yourself in a rolling swell of grey stone and cement, with domes delineating the vaults below. Freshly dyed fabric dries in the wind, creating a splash of colour. Only a faint buzz escapes from the vents in the roof to tell of the hubbub beneath your feet.

Bab Antakya

It's rewarding to ramble in the souks, but for a first visit you might follow the west-east axis from Bab Antakya (Antioch Gate) to the Citadel. Divert to left and right where temptation beckons, returning afterwards to the main route. Most of the old city wall has gone, but the western section survives, with the great bastions of Bab Antakya in the middle. It's about 600 m (660 yd) south of the museum and tourist information office, and further from most hotels—best to take a 39

ALEPPO

AD - DUDU

AS - SAFSAFAH

Park

Jib - al - Quebeh St.

Al - Abbassyen St.

AQIOL

Al - JIBELAH

Bab al - Hadid St.

Souk ar-Nahaseen

Al Kawakibi St.

An Nasri Hammam

Law Courts

CITADEL

The Great Mosque of the Citadel

AL - JDAIAH

QASTAL AL - HARAMI

AT - TIDRIBAH

QASTAL AL - MOSHT

Khan Qurshin

An Nasr Gate

Hammam as-Sultan

Qala'at

AL - FRAFIRAH

AL - AAJAM

AS - SIFAHIAH

Mousalam Ibn Abd al-Malek St.

Beit Ghazaleh

Beit Ajiqbash

Bab an Nasr St.

Jumblatt Palace

Abdul Moneim Riyad St.

Gold Souk

National Hospital

Khan an-Nahasin

Konnisin Gate

Clock Tower

Bab al-Faraj

AL - KHANDAK

AL - MOTANABBI St.

Great Mosque

Khan al-Gumtuk

Souk al-Attarin

AL - JALLOUM

Bab Antakya

Bab Qinnasrin

Tonsi St.

Nostaki St.

AL - AQABAH

Bab Antakya

Bab

Anfaksa

Aleppo Museum

Bus Station

Market

Az - Zalawi St.

Al - Maari St.

Baron St.

Al - Walid St.

Tourist Information Bureau

Fares - al - Khouri St.

Saad Allah al - Jaberee St.

Public Park

Al - Jalaa St.

Ibn Khaldun St.

Winter Sports Stadium

Ibrahim Hanano St.

Iskenderun St.

AL - JAMELAIAH

Al-Bohtori St.

Al - Godsi St.

ISMAAILIAH

Ibrahim Hanano Monument

AL - MASHARRAH

Souk al - Hal Street

N

0   950 m

taxi. Just inside the gate, make one of those diversions, up on to the top of the walls.

Souk al-Attarin

Back at ground level, after a couple of bends, the busy street becomes dead straight—it was the Roman *decumanus*, the main east-west street. Donkeys daintily pick their way among the crowds: they're much better suited to the narrow alleys than the pickup trucks that force their way through with horns blaring.

Khan al-Gumrok

Next to a high dome in the roof of the Souk al-Attarin, a gateway to the right leads to the biggest of Aleppo's many khans. The 1574 Khan al-Gumrok (or Customs House) became much more than an inn and warehouse for merchants: it was the headquarters of foreign trading companies, banks and consulates too. It is still a commercial hub, with scores of shops, offices on the upper level and a central mosque.

Khan al-Nahasin

The next big khan on the right was built for Venetian traders in the early 16th century. Its entrance is down a little side street, with an old but brightly modernized hammam (public bathhouse) opposite. Continue down this street to find on the left the decorative portal of Maristan Argun al-Kamil, an asylum for the insane built in 1354. Inside, little cells surround a pretty courtyard. The street ends at Bab Qinesrin, a restored gate in the city wall.

Great Mosque

North of the covered souks, the Great Mosque (or Mosque of Zachariah, father of John the Baptist) dates back to the beginnings of Islam. It was designed to the same pattern as the Omayyad Mosque in Damascus, but later alterations have produced a far less impressive building. The exception is the minaret, a square tower dating from 1090, with restrained decoration and fine Kufic inscriptions.

Citadel

The hill which dominates Aleppo was the site of the original settlement over 4,000 years ago. It may have started as a natural feature, growing higher as successive civilizations built on the ruins of their predecessors. The last to shape it were the Ayyubid rulers: Nur ed-Din, Salah ad-Din and his son Ghazi al-Malik. In their time the moat was dug and the face of the mound covered by a smooth stone glacis. Part of this survives, the stones prevented from slipping by Roman columns dug into the slope like pegs.

41

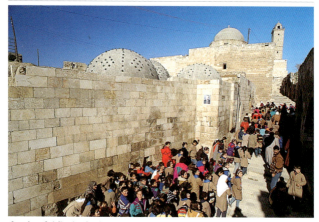

A colourful flock of schoolchildren exploring Aleppo's citadel.

The main gate is a masterpiece of military architecture, its survival remarkable since most of the citadel was destroyed long ago by invaders and earthquakes. The sloping bridge leads to the main tower, where five huge iron-plated doors set at angles could isolate any attackers and leave them exposed to a hail of arrows, rocks and boiling oil. They'd have had no time to appreciate the carved lintels, with serpents, lions and intricate Kufic script praising Allah the Merciful. High up in the tower is the restored throne room.

Inside the citadel remain traces of a Hittite temple, a Byzantine church converted into a mosque and part of the mosque built by Ghazi. Above all there's the view over the city, old and new, and a chance to get your bearings.

The streets to the north of the Citadel resound to the hammering of copper- and brass-beaters. And here you'll find that their modern successors—plumbers, heating engineers, car mechanics and recyclers of old tyres into pots and shoes—mainly stick together, one trade per street in the old way.

National Museum

The entrance is guarded by massive basalt statues from a temple at Tell Halaf, a 9th-century BC site in northeast Syria. Star exhibits are a great bronze lion and other statues from Mari, as well as some jewellery made of gold and semi-precious stones which would look superb if worn today. The objects from Tell Brak were excavated by Max Mallowan, the husband of Agatha Christie. There are finds from Ugarit, Ebla and from the rescue excavations of sites flooded by Lake Assad. Other rooms house delicate Byzantine glass and Islamic art, ceramics, glass and calligraphy.

Qalaat Semaan

In the 5th century, in the stony hills 40 km (25 miles) northwest of Aleppo, the ascetic Saint Simeon Stylites chose to spend the last 38 years of his life on top of a 16-m (53-ft) stone column, preaching to crowds of pilgrims whose numbers grew as his fame spread. Apparently he began by standing on a fairly low pillar, but he found that people could still climb up to touch him so he ordered the taller version, which in the event put him closer to heaven. After his death in 459, a vast and magnificent church was built, consisting of four basilicas in the form of a cross with the pillar as its focus. When the church was abandoned, collectors of holy relics and souvenir hunters chipped away at the pillar until almost nothing was left. Even the stump that you see now may not have been original. What is certain is that the church was an architectural masterpiece, innovative on the grand scale and in the lovely carved details of the honey-coloured stone.

Roman Road

As you come from Aleppo, just before the turn-off to Qalaat Semaan, the highway intersects a stretch of Roman road, 1,200 m (1,300 yd) long and well enough preserved to drive on today.

Dead Cities

Qalaat Semaan is only one of scores of "Dead Cities" scattered all over northern Syria, marked by their evocative churches, in ruins. Most were abandoned between the 8th and 10th centuries when war between the Byzantines and Arabs made settled life and agriculture on these marginal uplands untenable. It's possible to follow a circular route from Aleppo, visiting some of the sites along the way.

Cyrrhus, near the Turkish border, has the remains of a fine Roman theatre, even bigger than Bosra but far less well preserved. Near it on the road from Azaz, two 2nd-century Roman bridges are still in business carrying today's traffic.

43

PALMYRA (TADMOR)

Temple of Bel, Grand Colonnade, Tombs, Arab Castle, The Town

To romantics, Palmyra sounds like somewhere almost unattainably magical. It lies, in fact, 230 km (140 miles) northeast of Damascus, and 200 km (125 miles) southeast of Aleppo. You can reach it by good roads from Damascus, Homs or Deir ez-Zor and stay in a high-class hotel, but despite the modern incursions, much of the romance remains.

You drive for two or three hours, seeing no more evidence of human presence than a few Bedouin tents in the distance. The oasis appears quite suddenly: a grove of date palms, then the ruins—colonnades of honey-coloured stone, triumphal arches, temples and strange burial towers. Beyond them is the growing modern town of Tadmor (the ancient name); apart from tourism, there's a natural gas project in the area, phosphate mines and an airforce base.

Tablets from Mari dating from 1800 BC mention the oasis, but Palmyra's years of glory began after the Romans conveniently crushed its rivals, the Nabataeans, in AD 106. The Palmyrenes were left a measure of autonomy, and they grew rich on taxing the caravan trade. After the unfortunate Emperor Valerian was captured by the Persian Sassanids (whose king used him as a footstool!) Palmyra's prince, Odenathus, defeated the Sassanids in 263 and extended his rule over the whole of Syria and beyond. Four years later he was assassinated in Homs, and succeeded by his widow, the learned and beautiful Zenobia, who proclaimed herself queen of all the former Roman lands in Asia and Egypt.

In 272, the new Roman emperor, Aurelian, decided to restore imperial authority in the east. Zenobia defied him, but her army was beaten at Homs, and Palmyra surrendered after a siege. Captured trying to flee across the Euphrates, Zenobia was taken to Rome and led in golden chains in Aurelian's triumphal procession. The Palmyrenes rebelled and killed most of the garrison left by the emperor. In revenge, the Romans destroyed the city, and although they later restored it, the disruption caused by their continual wars with the Persians to the east led to its decline and eventual abandonment to the desert.

The Grand Colonnade is just a small part of the splendid site of Palmyra.

When two Englishmen, James Dawkins and Robert Wood, reached it in 1751, they found only a handful of Bedouin families living among the ruins. Two years later, they published *The Ruins of Palmyra* and caused a sensation: its detailed drawings inspired many an architectural or decorative feature in country houses and public buildings.

Temple of Bel

Bel (or Baal) was supreme among the Palmyrene gods—the Romans conveniently identified him with Jupiter—and this temple is the most massive building in the city. If the high plain wall extending 210 m (230 yd) on each side makes it look more like a fortress, that's because it was converted into one by the Arabs in the 12th century. Much later, the huge area inside was filled by the little houses and narrow alleyways of a village; it was cleared away in 1930.

The paved courtyard rises gently to the *cella* where the images of Bel and subordinate gods were kept and the sacred mysteries were performed. Unusually, the door is in one of the long sides.

Grand Colonnade

Starting at a triumphal arch, the east-west main street, more than 1,200 m (³/₄ mile) long unifies the vast site. The projecting consoles seen on many of the columns held statues of local worthies, a Palmyrene concept that disturbs the symmetry of the design and was repeated in few other places. Soon after the arch, you'll see the massive foundations of the Temple of Nebo, a Babylonian deity.

Theatre

On the same side as the Nebo temple, the restored theatre is used for performances in the Palmyra Festival. It looks small for such a great city, but that is because only about one-third of seats are left. They were long buried by sand, while the upper levels made a convenient quarry.

Tetrapylon

Where the colonnaded street makes a slight kink, four groups of four columns (all but one of the columns are restorations) form a prominent landmark. The open space to the south was the *agora*, or main square. Beyond the tetrapylon, the street continues, with the main part of the old city on the right. It finishes with a flourish at a six-columned burial vault that looks like a temple, at the point where another colonnade branches to the left. Beyond this is the site of the Diocletian Camp, the Roman army's quarters, and then the remains of the Roman wall.

Tombs

Scattered on the hillsides and along the valleys near Palmyra, scores of towers, mostly ruined, once contained floor upon floor of stone sarcophagi sealed into niches. Other tombs were built underground—the Three Brothers tomb is especially notable for its original wall paintings—and it seems certain that many of these have yet to be discovered. Each burial was marked with a sculpted likeness of the individual; most of these are now in museums. Women are often depicted drawing back their veils to display earrings and tiaras, men sometimes holding a goblet as if about to drink.

For the best light, visit the Valley of the Tombs west of the city at dawn, and return later to see inside the best-preserved tombs. They are kept locked, but you can join the tour beginning at 8.30 a.m. at the museum next to the town square.

Arab Castle

Credited to Saladin, but mainly built by Emir Fakhr el-Din in the early 17th century, the hilltop ruin of Qalaat ibn Maan looks far more impressive from afar than close-up, when the crude stonework contrasts painfully with the city spread below you. A moat and footbridge transversing it still exist, however diminished. It's worth driving up at sunset for the view, or if you'd rather see it in solitude, get there for sunrise.

The Town

The name Tadmor may come from the words for "city of dates", and indeed rows of stalls sell the delicious fruit from the oasis, especially in autumn. Small, round and delicious, they come in semi-dry golden-yellow and soft, red, sticky versions.

The gift shops offer the usual selections of crafts, Bedouin dresses, jewellery (not all old) and "antiques", the latter mostly made recently for the tourist market. You'll need to bargain hard to avoid paying inflated prices.

Museums

Opposite the Temple of Bel, the Museum of Popular Culture gives a good idea of the everyday life of the Bedouin people, both nomadic and settled. The rooms and activities of a house in the oasis as it might have been a few decades ago contrast with a Bedouin tent as it might still be today, although times are changing in the desert.

The Palmyra Museum on the square at the edge of the modern town has sculptures from the tombs and temples, a few mosaics and a striking model of the Temple of Bel showing the way it must have originally looked. 47

EUPHRATES VALLEY

Lake Assad, Resafa, Halabiyeh,
Deir ez-Zor, Doura Europos, Mari

Rising in Turkey, the river which nourished some of the world's most ancient civilizations crosses Syria for a distance of 500 km (310 miles) before entering Iraq and joining the Tigris. In the 8th and 9th centuries, when the Arab empire was at its zenith, norias like those at Hama lined the Euphrates (Al-Furat in Arabic), and its waters were channelled to fields, gardens and fountains. It was said that the Caliph could travel from Aleppo to Baghdad without leaving the shade of trees. Then the Mongols in the 13th century, and Timur (Tamerlane) in the 15th, destroyed the irrigation systems and the communities which tended them. The Ottoman Turks, for their part, simply neglected the valley.

Now prosperity is returning. With the building of the Al-Thawra Dam, water and electricity are reaching the villages and the cultivated area is rapidly expanding, growing wheat, cotton, maize, fruit and plantations of trees. Tractors and combine harvesters are everywhere, and there's an abundance of food. If you see an open-air market at one of the towns along the road, stop and pay a visit. It will be thronged with cheerful people, the women in vividly coloured dresses, the men in traditional robes. Find the sheep and goat market and you'll see a spectacle which can't have changed much in 2,000 years.

Lake Assad

The giant Al-Thawra ("Revolution") Dam on the Euphrates east of Aleppo generates enough electricity to power most of the country, and the lake it has created supplies water for irrigation. A new town has sprung up, with a viewing point where you can see the dam itself, stretching away into the distance.

Resafa

On the easterly road from Aleppo, a turning to the south at Al-Mansur heads from the river into the desert. After 25 km (16 miles), what looks at first like a mirage resolves into an imposing rectangle of walls, 2 km (over a mile) in perimeter, with round towers at each corner, and many smaller bastions. This is Resafa, the Byzantine city of Sergiopolis, named after St Sergius, a Roman army commander. One of Syria's own saints, he was tortured and martyred in about AD 300, when he proclaimed his Christianity and refused to make the official

Qalaat Jaabar enclosed by Lake Assad.

sacrifices to the Roman gods. Why was the Roman army here? It was a garrison town on the frontier facing the Sassanids to the east, as well as a staging post on the caravan route from Palmyra to the Euphrates. With the Christianization of the empire, Sergiopolis became a centre of pilgrimage. In the 6th century, the Emperor Justinian ordered the building of a great church and the mighty walls that still stand.

Crystal City

Arriving at the beautifully carved north gate, you begin to understand the secret behind Resafa's strange, ethereal appearance: almost everything is built of a crystalline gypsum rock. Sharp-edged, often rose-tinted and translucent when first cut, it turns a duller brown after exposure to the elements but keeps some of its shine. If you can resist the temptation to rush in through the gate, take the road round the outside of the walls first. A break at the southeast corner gives an overall view of the site: the countless little craters are the work of centuries of hopeful treasure hunters.

Southeast of the centre stands Justinian's basilica. Some of its majestic round arches—a reminder of Qalaat Semaan—were filled 49 in after an earthquake, and then part was turned into a mosque. The remains of a smaller basilica which may have been the first burial place of St Sergius stand to the south.

In the southwest corner of the walled city are three colossal vaulted cisterns, resembling underground cathedrals, designed to hold two years' supply of water. Be sure to watch your step: they're up to 20 m (66 ft) deep.

Halabiyeh

Beyond Raqqa—once one of the chief cities of the Arab empire but now rather unprepossessing —stand the ruins of the mightiest of the fortresses built by the Byzantines to protect their eastern frontier. First an outpost of Palmyra, it was taken over by the Romans when they crushed Queen Zenobia's bid for independence.

In the 6th century, Justinian reinforced the defences, but in AD 610 they fell to the Persians who went on to seize most of Syria and Egypt in a lightning campaign. When the Arab conquest followed, Halabiyeh was no longer on any frontier, and thus dropped out of history. Nor was there any nearby settlement to raid it for building materials, which accounts for its remarkable state of preservation after 14 centuries.

The site stands above the Euphrates, just off the road, to the north of Tibni. Look for a sign at the village of Shiha; then it's a 7-km (4-mile) drive along a narrow side road. From the river, huge walls reach up to the citadel, perched high on a pinnacle. The stone is the same crystalline gypsum used to build Resafa.

It's an aerobic scramble up the steep slope to the top, where you should take care not to fall into one of the holes that pepper the ruins. But the effort is repaid by the views along the river, away into the desert, and down within the walls where you can make out the plan of the Byzantine streets, the forum and a basilica.

Just upstream a pontoon bridge crosses the Euphrates. On the north bank, a dusty track between the railway and river leads to Halabiyeh's less impressive twin fort of Zalabiyeh.

Deir ez-Zor

The metropolis of the Euphrates valley is an agricultural centre and now an oil town, too—significant discoveries have been made in these parts after decades when it was assumed that Syria had no worthwhile quantities of oil. Deir ez-Zor's hotels, including one in the top category, make a good base for exploring the Euphrates valley and its sites, and a good road links it to Palmyra.

This is also camel country; herds can often be seen in the distance, or ambling across the road to new grazing grounds.

Doura Europos

The fortress-town, now Al-Salahiyeh, was founded by Alexander the Great's general, Seleucus, and later marked the Roman frontier with the Persians. Unlike Halabiyeh it was a trading centre as well as a military base, with a thoroughly mixed population to judge by the variety of temples, churches and a famous synagogue that once flourished. The Sassanid Persians besieged and eventually took Doura in AD 256. It was left in ruins and abandoned, until French archaeologists began to dig in the 1920s.

It stands on a strategic spot on a rocky cliff high above the Euphrates, easily spotted to the left of the main road as you head southeast. The Palmyra Gate is prominent, though you actually enter the town by way of a gap in the wall to the right of it. Just to your right are the remains of a Christian chapel, the earliest known in Syria. Close to the wall on the other side of the Palmyra Gate was the original site of a synagogue with splendid wall-paintings now in the National Museum in Damascus. Straight ahead from the gate was the main street; pick your way across the city and you'll be rewarded by a view of the Seleucid citadel, standing on a separate pinnacle of rock above the Euphrates. Major restorations and archaeological work are going on in this part of the site.

Mari

Excavations have identified the mound known as Tell Hariri, 25 km (16 miles) south of Doura Europos (not far from the frontier with Iraq), as the Bronze Age city of Mari. A kingdom which prospered on river trade, it flourished from 3000 BC to about 1750 BC, when it fell to Hammurabi, King of Babylon.

Mari was first excavated by the French archaeologist André Perrot following the chance discovery of a statue in 1933. Mud-brick buildings were revealed, so massive that walls up to 5 m (16 ft) high survived into modern times. Some of them bore elaborate wall-paintings, now preserved in the national museums in Damascus and Aleppo, along with superb jewellery, statues and many cuneiform tablets telling of the commercial and diplomatic life of those days. The much-dug site today is confusing, with little sign of its former glories.

Note that the area may sometimes be closed for security reasons, because of its proximity to the Iraq border.

Cultural Notes

Entertainment

If you came to Syria for the nightlife, you can expect to be disappointed. In Damascus the British, French, German and Russian cultural centres sometimes put on concerts by visiting artists, and the ancient theatres at Palmyra and Bosra are used for performances in their annual festivals. The big hotels might stage a folkdance show, none too authentic, or a cabaret with an Egyptian belly-dancer. The favourite local form of relaxation, but strictly for the men, is to sit in a coffee house for hours playing backgammon (*taouli* or *shishbesh* in Arabic). Every town has at least one big, brightly lit café packed with players, most of them smoking a *narghileh*, a water-cooled tobacco pipe. In a few, they're entertained by a traditional story-teller. The women, meanwhile, are at home chatting or watching television.

The Islamic Year

The Muslim calendar has twelve months, but as they are determined by the phases of the moon, the total number of days is eleven less than the Western year based on the sun. Thus Ramadan begins eleven days earlier each year, by the Western calendar. When it falls in the long hot days of summer, its restrictions are especially onerous.

The years are numbered from the Hegira, the flight of Mohammed from Mecca to Medina in AD 622. The Islamic year AH 1417 began in May 1997. But except for determining Muslim festivals and holidays, Syria works to the Western calendar, so you won't have to worry about converting dates.

Mancala

Keep your eyes open at the ancient sites and you'll soon spot them—double rows of holes chipped into horizontal stone surfaces. In the paving of the Temple of Bel at Palmyra, in the seats of the Roman theatre at Bosra, high on the ramparts of Crusader castles, these are boards for playing mancala (*manqala* in Arabic, from the verb "to move"). It is probably the world's oldest board game. Boards have even been found in Egyptian tombs dating from 1500 BC. The game spread all over the Islamic world from Indonesia to West Africa, where it's called *wari*, and crossed the Atlantic with the slaves.

So how do you play? There are at least as many variations of the game as countries, but here is one version popular in Syria, where the board usually has two rows of seven holes.

There are two players, one on each side of the board. The first player spreads 96 beans round the 14 holes, any way he likes but putting at least 4 in each hole. The other picks up all the beans from one of the holes on his side, and drops ("sows") them, one per hole in the following holes, taken anti-clockwise, until they are all used. If the last bean makes a total of 2 or 4 in that hole, that player picks up those beans. Together with the beans in the hole opposite, if they add up to 2 or 4. If the preceding hole has 2 or 4, they are also picked up, and the hole opposite, and so on.

The first player now moves in the same way. They take turns until neither is able to move. The player with the most beans at that stage wins. Needless to say, there's scope for strategy, tactics—and sharp practice.

Sign Language

A lot of communication in the Arab world is by gesture. A slight raising of the eyebrows and simultaneous tilting back of the head means "No". It may not look emphatic, but it probably is. An outstretched hand, palm up, wrist twisting so the hand rocks from side to side, means "What are you looking for?" or "What do you want?" This is a sign used by cruising taxi drivers to drum up business. An arm reaching towards you, palm down, in a patting motion, means "Come with me" (not "stay there", as you might think).

Spell Check

There has never been much consistency when converting Arabic words to Roman script. Attempts at "rational" schemes have merely resulted in yet another set of options. Is that town southeast of Damascus Suweida, Swaida, Suwaida, Swayda, Sweydah? Is Syria's chief port Lattakia, Latakia, Lattakieh, Lattakiyeh, Lattakié, Lattaquié? The chick-pea purée which features in a *mezze (meze, mezzeh)*, is it *hommus, hommos, hummus, hummous*? All of those are acceptable, and you'll probably see other versions, too. Part of the problem is that written Arabic usually omits vowels, and in spoken Arabic, many vowel sounds are a general-purpose "uh", not quite an a, e, i, o or u!

A similarly cavalier attitude prevails among Syrian sign-writers concerning English spelling: SAF JURNY!, POLIEC CENTER, ESTERNE ANTIKS, WELL COME! 53

Shopping

Syria's artisans have always been famed for their skills, especially its metalworkers and weavers—the very words damascening and damask derive from Damascus. Their training is still rigorous and they continue to produce work of the highest quality. Except in a fixed-price store, you will have to haggle.

Where to Shop

The souks of Damascus and Aleppo may be stuffed with plastics, cheap fabrics and cassettes these days, but they are still happy hunting grounds for traditional craft work. At the crafts centre next door to the Tekiyeh Mosque in Damascus you can see a whole range of products; prices are fixed, so if you don't enjoy bargaining, this is the place to shop. Here and elsewhere, you can see weavers in action, and glassblowers in their oven-like workshops, turning out flasks, vases and lamps in green and a vivid turquoise. Then there are the traditional chequered Arab headcloths (*kefiyeh*) and "hubble-bubble" water pipes (*narghileh*). Impractical, yes, but absolutely irresistible.

Marquetry and Veneer

Ornate backgammon and chess boards, boxes and even large items of furniture are inlaid with rosewood and bone, highlighted with mother-of-pearl. Prices and quality vary widely, so inspect each one closely. In the mass-produced versions, fine mosaic patterns are made by gluing rods of wood and bone together in a bunch. Dozens of thin cross-sections are then sliced from the bunch and applied to a board as a veneer.

Old and New

Unusual bygones can turn up on the dusty shelves of souvenir shops, and if you show an interest you'll be surprised at the strange and perhaps valuable objects the shopkeeper will bring out. But remember, the traditional crafts are very much alive. There may be no way you can tell if a piece of Bedouin jewellery was made 200 years ago or last week.

The same applies to antiquities; the fine art of faking has been around so long it's practically respectable. At the famous sites—Palmyra, Apamea, Bosra —you can expect to be offered statuettes, coins and other attractive little items that the seller (looking furtively around) claims to have dug up himself at night. Maybe, but probably not. If you are tempted, remember: (a) it would be illegal to dig, sell, buy or export genuine antiquities without a licence; (b) they know the market price of the real thing, and if they did find anything desirable it would go to a dealer, not be hawked around to tourists as a bargain. That convincing "silver" Seleucid coin would turn brown in your pocket before you got it home. On the other hand a copper coin of Constantine the Great might be genuine—they're two a penny and not worth faking anyway.

Metalwork

Copper and brass are hammered into pots, planters and trays. Some are then engraved with fine designs, or etched with acid, a cheaper process.

The medieval swordsmiths of Damascus were famous for their blades, diamond-hard, mirror-smooth and inlaid with gold and silver wire (the process of damascening). You can still find some of the same work, though the best is expensive.

If the gold bangles, bracelets and earrings that glitter in the gold souks take your fancy, you can buy with confidence. Items are hallmarked for purity and sold by weight; there's little scope for bargaining.

Weaving and Embroidery

Damask fabrics first came from China but they have been woven in Damascus for almost a thousand years. The technique leaves the warp threads on one side of several weft threads, instead of interweaving every thread. This creates a sheen in those areas, catching the light to give the illusion of a sculptured effect.

Brocades, another speciality, have *extra* weft threads carried to the front of the weave, giving a genuinely raised effect. They often use the richest colours, along with gold and silver threads, to make traditional designs called *damasco*, *aghabani*, *dima* and *kashmir*.

Bedouin women's dresses may be simply embroidered in red cross-stitch on plain black cotton, or densely covered with intricate needlework. Generally the design is characteristic of an area or tribe, but it takes an expert to tell.

Decorative chain-stitched tablecloths are stacked up by the thousand in the souks, but don't despise them on that account. With matching napkins they'll give a festive look to your dining table.

55

Dining Out

Syrian food reflects the influences of its neighbours and its history. A close resemblance to Lebanese cuisine (more familiar in the West) is not surprising; the two countries were virtually one until 1920. And since both were part of the Ottoman Empire for centuries, you'll find dishes—kebabs, yoghurts—that remind you of Turkey. The Arab heritage shows up in the flat bread and the love of ultra-sweet things often perfumed with floral essences.

Mezze

Middle-Eastern hors d'œuvres may consist of two or three dishes, or a table laden with thirty or forty. This *is* intended as a preliminary, but may be so copious and tempting that you will leave no room for a main course. Just remember that it is not obligatory to finish, or even to try, all of the dishes in the *mezze*.

They may include *hummus*, a purée of chick peas with sesame oil, lemon and garlic, eaten by scooping it up with small pieces of flat Arab bread *(khobz)*. The same technique is used with *babaghanouj*, made from aubergine (eggplant) puréed with garlic and oil, and garnished with mint and pomegranate seeds. *Moutabbal* is a sharper version, made with yoghurt. More mezze components might be stuffed vine leaves, spicy meat balls, lambs' brains, liver and other items of offal.

Cracked wheat, or *burghul*, figures in several national dishes. In *kibbeh* it is mixed with minced (ground) lamb, onions and spices; *tabbouleh* is a refreshing salad of cracked wheat with finely chopped parsley, mint, onion, tomato and lemon juice.

Main Courses

Lamb and chicken are the basis of most main dishes. *Shish-kebab* in Syria means minced lamb, pressed into small patties and grilled on skewers. *Shashlik* is a kebab of small pieces of lamb, marinated in various spices. *Shish taouk* is similar but using chicken. Spit-roasted chicken is a universal stand-by, half a small chicken *(nus farooj)* being the usual portion, with optional garlic purée and Arab bread.

56

Street stands in every town sell *shwarma*, lamb formed into a cone shape, impaled on a spit, mounted vertically and rotated slowly before a brazier. Servings are then carved with a flourish from the outside with a sharp knife and pushed into a pocket of flat bread, with optional parsley and mint. It's wise to make sure your portion of meat is well-cooked.

One staple that appears on snack stalls and in the everyday diet, *falafel* is fried balls of chickpea paste with spices and pickled vegetables served on flat bread.

Small, fried, bony fish of the mullet family are the usual offering at restaurants along the coast.

The more expensive hotels run restaurants with "international" menus, but luckily they also feature the local favourites—which they tend to do better.

Desserts

The local sweet tooth is more than catered for in a whole range of calorific concoctions. *Baklava* is a delicious fine filo pastry filled with nuts and soaked with a honey solution, and *kounafa*, another dentist's nightmare, resembles "shredded wheat" soaked in honey. Most western palates can't take more than one or two pieces of these Arabian delights, so it's a relief to find plenty of fresh fruit.

Drinks

Coffee *(ahwe)* is concentrated and black, unless you ask for "Nescafé" (the generic term for instant). Usually flavoured with cardamom, it's served in tiny cups or glasses that allow no more than two or three sips before you encounter a thick sediment of grounds. It comes heavily sugared unless you ask for *mazboot* (medium) or *saada* (unsweetened). Tea *(shai)* is even more popular, served without milk; sugar is optional.

Wines are produced in Syria, but they have yet to make a name for themselves for quality or consistency. A thin red, a white and a rosé are available: for something better try the Lebanese, Cyprus, or occasional Hungarian, Italian or (expensive) French wines. Arak is an aniseed-flavoured spirit, rather like Greek ouzo or Pernod. It's the local favourite to go with a mezze, and drunk diluted with water which makes it turn milky. Locally brewed beer is weak and watery. The better hotels stock imported brands, notably Tuborg and Carlsberg.

Non-carbonated mineral water, available everywhere, comes from two different mountain sources, Boukein and Dreikich. Some of the international soft drink brands are bottled in Syria, but best of all are the freshly squeezed fruit juices.

The Hard Facts

To help you plan your trip, here are some of the practical details you should know about Syria.

Airports

Damascus International Airport lies 29 km (18 miles) southeast of the city. There are buses to the city centre, and taxis are always available. The journey takes about 30 minutes.

Check-in for international flights is two hours before the flight time. A departure tax is charged, payable in local currency—ask at your hotel to find out the current amount. Flight information is available 24 hours a day; tel. 543-0200.

Baggage

On most flights, you are allowed to check in 20 kg (44 lb). One carry-on bag is permitted.

Car Rental

Hiring a car is a convenient way of getting around, and reasonably economical. Some of the international companies are represented in Syria, and it may be worth making a reservation through one of them in your home country, before your visit. There are also good local companies. Check that

rates include full insurance against loss and damage. There is normally a charge per kilometre travelled above a certain daily average, but unlimited distance rates are also quoted. There may be an extra charge for drop-off at a different location, and for additional driver(s).

To rent a car, you need to hold a valid driving licence and an International Driving Licence and to be over 21 (25 with some companies). You are expected to pay with a major credit card.

Climate

Summers are hot and humid on the coast (although there is scarcely any rain), hot and dry inland, reaching day temperatures of over 45°C (113°F) in summer. Winters are cool, with occasional rain, especially in the mountains, where snow is also quite common, but there can be warm sunny days, too. Spring is the best time for a visit, followed by autumn.

Clothing

Take lightweight clothing in summer (cotton is most comfortable), with an extra layer for cool evenings. A raincoat, or at least an umbrella, will be useful in winter and spring.

A few formal restaurants require men to wear a jacket and tie.

Communications

The telephone system is being modernized and generally works well. The outgoing international code is 00. You can make calls from telecommunications offices, where you can also buy cards for card-operated phones (there's even one in the Temple of Bel in Palmyra!). It generally costs much more to call from your hotel room, unless you use one of the calling cards issued by international telephone companies. Fax messages can be sent and received through a few top hotels.

Cautious steps are being taken to allow Syrians internet access. You may be able to check e-mails at major hotels.

Crime

Syria is one of the world's safest countries for travellers. Street crime is almost unknown, but it's sensible to take normal precautions: beware of pickpockets in crowded places, leave valuables in the hotel safe, lock your car when parking and don't leave desirable things on show.

Driving

You need a national driving licence and also an International Driving Licence, obtained from one of the motoring organizations in your home country. Roads are generally adequate but may be potholed in places. Drive on the right. Speed limits for cars are 80 kph outside towns, 110 kph on the *autostrada* (motorway) and otherwise as marked.

Be prepared for people and animals in the road at any time, and for other drivers to do surprising things, stopping or turning suddenly without warning. Make sure your horn is working, and use it. Don't drive at night: many vehicles carry no rear lights, or no lights at all.

If you have an accident, try to inform the police, or ensure that someone else does. If anyone is injured, you may be arrested until blame is allocated.

Petrol and diesel fuel are available, and cheap by European standards, but filling stations may be far apart; fill up before starting an out-of-town journey. Check oil, water and tyres before a long desert crossing.

Emergencies

To call the Police dial 112; Traffic Police 115; the Fire Service 113; an Ambulance 110. Do not expect the respondent to understand English.

Essentials

Be sure to take sunscreen cream (a high protection factor is essential except in winter), a sun hat, dark glasses, insect repellent, a torch (flashlight), spare batteries, binoculars, film, lipsalve (the desert air is very dry) and any medicines you may need—the same brands may not be available.

Etiquette

Dress modestly: shorts and other revealing clothes are not appreciated.

Always greet someone before asking a question or saying anything else. Shake hands when meeting people, and when taking leave. One exception: you should not try to shake hands with a woman wearing a veil or headscarf.

Use only the right hand for giving anything, and for handling food. Don't show the soles of your feet or shoes; it's considered impolite.

It's courteous to accept coffee or tea when it is offered, and to accept a second cup. (But there's no need to take coffee with every shopkeeper who offers it—or to buy anything if you do.)

Formalities

Visas, valid for a visit of up to 15 days, are required by travellers from almost all countries (other Arab countries are an exception). The visa should be obtained in advance from the Syrian embassy in your home country. Allow at least a week for it to be issued. A photograph is needed and a substantial fee is charged.

Local and foreign currency may be imported, but it is forbidden to export Syrian money. You may import duty-free the following: 200 cigarettes or 25 cigars or 250 g tobacco; half a litre of spirits; 30 g perfume for personal use and half a litre eau de toilette.

Carry your passport with you at all times. Hotels will ask for it when you check in, and may want to keep it overnight, at least for the first night.

Health
and Medical Matters

After a long flight, relax for a couple of days. Doctors suggest eating lightly, and avoiding too much sun. In hot weather, drink plenty of water, wear a sunhat, use a sunscreen with a high protection factor (at least 20) and make sure that children do the same.

Except in the top hotels, avoid salads—even green garnishes and snacks such as radishes which are grown in unhygienic conditions.

There is a slight risk of malaria in the northern border areas and Euphrates valley from May to October. Typhoid, cholera, tetanus and hepatitis vaccinations are recommended. Rabies is endemic; if bitten by any animal, get immediate medical attention. Pharmacies sell a wide variety of medications, including prescription drugs, but some will be under unfamiliar names.

It is highly advisable to take out comprehensive travel insurance, including coverage of medical expenses.

Languages
Arabic is the national language; English is quite widely understood and there is a considerable legacy of French in educated circles. Try to learn and use a few polite phrases in Arabic—your efforts will be greatly appreciated.

Media
Radio, TV and printed media are under government control. The *Syria Times*, a daily newspaper in English, carries a limited amount of international news, and lists the times of Syrian radio and TV programmes in English, French and other non-Arabic languages. Imported newspapers and magazines are subject to official censorship.

Money
The currency is the Syrian pound or *lira*, £S (or SYP). It is nominally divided into 100 piastres, but in practice only paper money from £S5 to 1000 is in general use.

Foreign currency and travellers cheques may be changed at branches of Syria Commercial Bank, exchange offices and large hotels; all give the same rate. You may be offered a little more by unofficial dealers but such transactions are illegal.

Hotel rooms must be paid for in US dollars except in the very cheapest places. Restaurant and other bills can be paid for in local money. Only the top-grade hotels take credit cards, and the bill will be in dollars. It's worth taking a supply of US dollars, especially smaller denominations ($1, $5, $10) with you to Syria, and always carrying some. It may be hard to change $50 and $100 bills, and many forgeries exist.

Opening Hours
Museums generally open from 9 a.m. to about 4 p.m. Most close on Tuesday, and for an hour or two at midday on Friday. Archaeological sites are mostly open from 8.30 a.m. to 4 or 5 p.m. daily (later in summer).

Shops open from 9 or 10 a.m. to 2 p.m., and again from 4 or 4.30 p.m. to 8 or 9 p.m. Most are closed on Friday. Business and government offices and post offices operate from 8 or 8.30 a.m. to 2 or 2.30 p.m., except on Friday. Banks open from 8 or 9 a.m. to 1 or 2 p.m., except Friday. Exchange offices keep longer hours.

Photography and Video

Avoid photographing "sensitive" subjects—military or industrial installations, infrastructure such as important bridges, and areas close to international borders. Ask permission before taking photos of people, and respect any reluctance they may show. Men are usually happy to be photographed—in country areas they may call their friends to get into the picture too.

Colour print film is widely available in the cities; transparency film is hard to find. Colour prints can be processed locally but quality cannot be guaranteed. Transparency film is best taken back to your own country for processing.

Video-tape is available. Pre-recorded tapes are compatible with most of Europe, but not the US.

Public Holidays

January 1	New Year's Day
March 8	Revolution Day
April 17	Independence Day
May 1	Labour Day
May 6	Martyrs' Day
December 25	Christmas

Moveable: Muslim
Muslim New Year
Prophet's Birthday

Beginning of Ramadan
Id al-Fitr (end of Ramadan, 3 days)
Id al-Adha (3 days)
Moveable: Christian
Easter Sunday (Western)
Easter Sunday (Orthodox)

Public Transport

State and private bus companies run regular services connecting all the main cities and towns, starting from central bus stations or the company's own terminal. Cheaper buses and minibuses operate on the "service" system, waiting until they are full before departing, and stopping anywhere along a fixed route to drop off and pick up passengers. "Service" taxis are a comfortable and quick alternative, but much more expensive. Within cities, taxis are readily available and inexpensive. If they don't have meters, agree the fare in advance.

Trains, usually only one per day, run on two main lines: from Damascus to Aleppo, Deir ez-Zor and Qamishle in the northeast; and from Aleppo to the Mediterranean coastal towns (Lattakia, Tartus), Homs and Damascus.

Internal flights connect Damascus and Aleppo, and both of these cities to Qamishle.

Religion

The vast majority (well over 80 per cent) of people are Muslim, most of them Sunnis but with minorities from the Shia and the influential Alawi sects. A small group belong to the Druze religion, an offshoot of Islam. The remainder, about 13 per cent, are Christians of many different sects, such as the Greek Orthodox, Syrian Orthodox, Roman Catholic, Greek Catholic, Maronite, Armenian and various Protestant churches. Of the once-large Jewish community, most have long since emigrated, but a few still live in Damascus.

When visiting a mosque, you are expected to dress modestly and to remove your shoes. Carry them if there is nowhere to leave them.

Time

Syria is on GMT + 2, advancing one hour from April to September. Thus for most of the year it is one hour ahead of most of western Europe and two hours ahead of the UK and Ireland.

Tipping

Waiters and taxi-drivers expect a tip of about 10 per cent. They may add it to the bill themselves, and deduct the appropriate amount—as they see it—from your change. Be sure to count. Even where restaurant bills include service, your waiter will still expect an additional cash tip of 5 to 10 per cent.

Toilets

The better hotels have Western-type facilities. Otherwise, toilets are the hole-in-the-ground version, usually clean and with a tap and short hosepipe for flushing, but often lacking paper.

Tourist Information

The airport at Damascus and most major towns have a tourist office, open from 9 a.m. to 1 or 2 p.m., and sometimes from 4 p.m. to 7 p.m., except Friday. The literature they have available is often very limited: some can provide you with a map of the local area. Syrian embassies abroad have some tourist information including maps.

Voltage

The electrical supply is 220V, 50 Hz, AC. Plugs are of the mainland European type, with two round pins. Any 110V equipment needs a transformer as well as an adaptor. Power may be cut off occasionally; large hotels have their own generators.

Water

Tap water is safe to drink in the main towns and cities, although many people prefer the good local bottled spring water—check that the seal is unbroken. Drink bottled water in remote areas—carry your own supply where possible.

INDEX

GENERAL EDITOR
Barbara Ender-Jones
EDITOR
Alice Taucher
LAYOUT
Luc Malherbe
PHOTO CREDITS
Hemisphères/Lechenet: front cover
Pascal Herren: pp. 1, 8
PRISMA: pp. 19, 26
Bernard Joliat: pp. 23, 30, 38, 45, 49
MAPS:
Elsner & Schichor
JPM Publications

Copyright © 2005, 1998
by JPM Publications S.A.
12, avenue William-Fraisse,
1006 Lausanne, Switzerland
E-mail:
information@jpmguides.com
Web site:
http://www.jpmguides.com/

Printed in Switzerland – 05/05/01
Weber/Bienne
Edition 2005–2006